# Katy Perry

young
reader's
library of  pop
biographies

Adele

Katy Perry

Lady Gaga

Macklemore

Nicki Minaj

young
reader's
library of **pop
biographies**

# Katy Perry

C. F. Earl

**Young Reader's Library of Pop Biographies:
Katy Perry**

Village Earth Press
Vestal, New York 13850
www.villageearthpress.com

First Printing
9 8 7 6 5 4 3 2 1

Series ISBN (paperback): 978-1-62524-441-3
ISBN (paperback): 978-1-62524-390-4
ebook ISBN: 978-1-62524-146-7
          Library of Congress Control Number: 2014933985

Author: Earl, C. F.

# Table of Contents

# Chapter One

# At the Top, Looking Back

**A**t the 2013 MTV Video Music Awards, Katy Perry was ready to give her fans their first taste of her newest music. After Katy had taken over the world with her album *Teenage Dream*, her fans were hungry for more from the superstar singer.

Katy was about to perform her newest song, "Roar." Although the song would soon become her biggest hit, before Katy took the stage that night, her fans had never heard it.

The stage was made up to look like a boxing ring. Katy performed dressed as a boxer, wearing shiny shorts and boxing gloves. "Roar" is about fighting against the odds and staying strong when things are tough, so Katy's boxing costume matched the song's message perfectly.

Her huge performance at the MTV VMAs showed Katy's millions of fans that she was going to give them more amazing music. Today, Katy Perry is one of the biggest music stars in the world. Few singers have had as much success as Katy has had. She's had huge hit songs and sold millions of albums. Katy's known all over the world for her big voice and exciting, colorful style.

Of course Katy wasn't always a superstar! She started out as a little girl who grew up living a very different life.

# EARLY LIFE

Katy Perry's real name is Katheryn Elizabeth Hudson. She was born on October 25, 1984 outside Santa Barbara, California. Katy's parents are Mary Christine and Maurice Keith Hudson. Katy's parents were **Pentecostal** pastors. They traveled around the United States setting up new churches, taking Katy and her brother and sister with them. Soon, though, the family came back to Santa Barbara to stay. For most of her life, Katy has lived in her home state of California.

**Pentecostal** Christians are a group of Christians who believe strongly that baptism and accepting Jesus are needed to go to heaven. They place a special emphasis on a direct personal experience of God through what they refer to as the "baptism of the Holy Spirit," which they believe produces supernatural signs such as "speaking in tongues," visions, or miraculous healings.

In 2013, Katy talked to National Public Radio (NPR) about growing up in a religious household. "I was never allowed to call deviled eggs 'deviled eggs,' I called them 'angel eggs,'" the singer said. Katy's parents were strict about what was allowed in their house, so Katy's life was very different from the lives of other girls her age. She even told Vanity Fair magazine that she didn't feel like she had a childhood because of all her parents' rules. "I come from a very non-accepting family, but I'm very accepting," she said.

Things were tough sometimes for Katy growing up. Her parents loved her, but they kept a tight hold on her. Katy loved to sing, but her parents didn't allow many types of music in the house. She wasn't allowed to listen to pop, rock, or rap. Instead, she listened to gospel music and older music her parents liked. For the most part, any music that wasn't religious was kept away from Katy when she was young.

Still, Katy loved music, and she sang in church as much as she could. Singing in church gave Katy practice for her future and allowed her to get better and better. She got a guitar for her birthday when she was thirteen, and after that, she started writing her own songs.

Katy's young life was very different from the star fans know today. She told NPR: "I think that parents grow up with an idea of what they want their kids to be like—and then their kids grow up to be people of themselves, of their own."

## STARTING IN MUSIC

When Katy was fifteen years old, she finished high school early—and then she and her mother went to Nashville, Tennessee. Katy and her parents had visited the city a few times, and Katy had sung in a church there. Some Nashville musicians had heard her, and now they wanted to work with her on the songs she had been writing. Nashville was a good place for Katy to get a start in the music world. The city has been the center of the country music business for decades.

Katy arrived in Nashville ready to chase her dreams of making music. She started working with rock and country musicians. She learned to play guitar and write better songs. She practiced every day, working to become the best she could. Katy started recording her own gospel music. She had always loved the music—and now she was making her own album.

Years later, Katy talked to MTV News about her time in Nashville: "I'd actually have to superglue the tips of my fingers because

Nashville, Tennessee, shown here, has a long, rich musical history. Being surrounded by that culture helped Katy grow as a musician.

## Music History: Nashville, Tennessee

For years, Nashville has been one of America's most important musical cities. The city has been home to a huge part of the country music business all the way back to the earliest days of country music. In many ways, Nashville is a city built around music. It is filled with the sound of music coming from bars and theatres. Seeing live music is a big part of having a good time in Nashville. People come from around the world to see a city with a special place in music history. Today, the city is still the heart of a huge amount of country music and even pop music. Stars like Taylor Swift, Jack White, and the Black Keys have all worked in the musical city of Nashville.

they hurt so much from playing guitar all day. And from that, I made the best record I could make as a gospel singer at fifteen."

In 2001, Katy finished her album *Katy Hudson*. A small record **label** put out the album, and it didn't sell very well. Katy's songs were played on the radio, though, and it was good practice for her.

Soon, Katy and her mother were headed back to Santa Barbara, California. Today, Katy looks back on her time in Nashville as great training for the life she would soon be leading as one of the world's most famous musical artists. Things might not have worked out for Katy Hudson's musical career—but soon Katy Perry's success would make up for it.

A record **label** is a company that publishes music.

# Find Out Even More

Want to find out more about Katy Perry? The library is a good place to get started. Books that tell the story of one person's life are called biographies. This book that you're reading right now is a biography of Katy Perry's life. No one book can hold all the information there is to know about a singer like Katy, though. Writers have to make choices about what to include in a book and what to leave out. Other authors may include other details. They may emphasize different parts of her story. Reading a biography like this one will give you lots of information about her life—but reading more than one book about Katy could get you a fuller picture of her life and music.

Try finding some of the books listed below:

Bernard, Jan. *Katy Perry (Stars of Today)*. North Mankato, MN: The Child's World Inc., 2012.

Frisch, Aaron. *Katy Perry (The Big Time)*. Mankato, MN: The Creative Company, 2011.

Friedlander, Noam. *Katy Perry*. New York, Sterling, 2012.

If you can't find these books, see if your library has other biographies of Katy. You can use the card catalog or the library's computers to find books about Katy—or ask a librarian for help. Then take a look through one of the books you've found and ask yourself the following questions:

1. How helpful is the table of contents? Try finding a chapter that sounds interesting to you and flip to that page. Take a look at the chapter. Could you tell by the title of the chapter what it would be about? Does it offer interesting information?
2. How is the book organized? Does the book tell the story of Katy's life in the order that things happened? Does it organize her life in a different way? Does it rely on photographs more than text—or is it mostly words, with very few pictures? Is it somewhere in between? How much time does it spend on her childhood? Does it focus more on her music than her life? There are no right or wrong answers to these questions, but each one will help you decide if the book you're looking at is one you want to read.
3. Can you use the index to find topics in the book that interest you? Look over the index until you find a subject you want to learn more about and flip to the first page where it appears. How helpful was the index in finding something interesting?
4. After you read the book, ask yourself what you thought about it. Did you like the book? Why or why not? Does this book contain facts or stories you couldn't find in somewhere else? Was it interesting? Did you learn something new?

# Chapter Two

# Katy Lives Her Dream

After creating a gospel album as a teenager, Katy was headed in a different direction just a few years later. This time, she followed her music dreams to Los Angeles, and this time she went by herself, without her mother. In her new home, she took on a new name to start a new career in music. She chose to perform now under the name Katy Perry, because her mother's maiden name is Perry.

Katy had the name that she'd make famous. Now she would have to spend a long time working hard to become the star fans know today.

## WORKING HER WAY TO THE TOP

In L.A., Katy worked with music producer Glen Ballard to become a better songwriter and a better artist. Glen had worked with famous artists like Alanis Morissette, Dave Matthews, and

No Doubt. He saw something in Katy. He knew she could be a star, too. Glen worked closely with Katy to help her learn more about the business of making music and writing pop songs.

Life in Los Angeles was very different from life in Santa Barbara when Katy was growing up. Katy was on her own now, away from her parents' supervision, and she was free to live how she wanted. She experienced new things and met people who didn't think like her parents or the other people she knew growing up. Katy has said that moving to L.A. opened her eyes to new things, including new kinds of music.

Over the next few years, a few different record labels wanted to work with Katy to produce her music. She signed record **contracts** with a few labels, but in the end, they all dropped her. At one point, she had an album almost finished, but then the label decided not to put the album out after all and dropped Katy from the label. For a young artist like Katy just trying to be heard, it was hard to hear "no" again and again.

In 2007, Capitol Records signed Katy and starting working with her to put together a new album. Finally, Katy would get a chance to show the world her new music.

**Contracts** are written agreements between people or companies.

Katy talked to website BlogCritics.com about her journey in the music business before she found success: "It took five years. It wasn't overnight. It was five years of major labels being signed and dropped, signed and dropped." She went on to say, "You know, I think the advantage of that was that I really got to grow. Also, I got to work with so many different people and take my

## Music History: The *Billboard* Charts

*Billboard* magazine began publishing entertainment news in 1894. At first, the magazine showed people where they could find the latest artistic performances and fun activities. Later, the magazine focused more on music. In the 1930s, *Billboard* started tracking the most popular music of the time, ranking songs on charts. Each kind of music had its own chart in the magazine, with the most popular music reaching the top spot. For decades, getting a number-one song on the *Billboard* charts has been a sign of success for artists and music companies. Today, Katy Perry has more number-one hits than many of the most famous musicians and singers in music. With song after song, Katy has proven that she's an important voice in pop music.

time and really kind of carve out and figure out who I was and what I wanted to say...as an artist."

Katy had to gotten so close so many times, only to have a record deal after record deal fall apart. She was afraid to hope that this time would be different. Soon, though, her hard work would pay off, and she'd find a whole new level of success in music.

## ONE OF THE BOYS

In the summer of 2008, Katy released *One of the Boys*. The album was her first with her new name Katy Perry. The new album, new look, and new sound would make Katy a superstar.

Making the switch from gospel to pop music wasn't easy for Katy—but it paid off in the end!

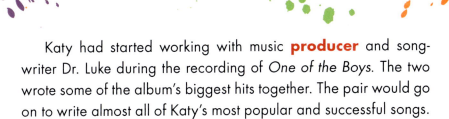

Katy had started working with music **producer** and song-writer Dr. Luke during the recording of *One of the Boys*. The two wrote some of the album's biggest hits together. The pair would go on to write almost all of Katy's most popular and successful songs.

The first **single** from *One of the Boys*, "I Kissed a Girl," helped Katy get people's attention. The song became an almost immediate hit when it came out. Not long after its **release**, the song hit the number-one spot on the *Billboard* Hot 100 pop songs chart. This chart is one of the biggest ways the success of a song is measured. With "I Kissed a Girl," Katy reached a huge number of people and gained many new fans. Soon, everyone was talking about the new singer named Katy Perry.

After the success of "I Kissed a Girl," Katy put out her next single, "Hot n Cold." The song was another major hit for Katy. It broke into the top five on the *Billboard* Hot 100 chart, but it didn't make it to number one. The song helped Katy make sure people knew she wasn't just a singer with one hit song, though. She could keep making great music. The album's next single, "Thinking of You," didn't do as well as the first two, but "Waking Up in Vegas" was a smash hit on radio, music television, and online.

After all of Katy's hard work she could hardly

A **producer** is a person in charge of recording music and turning it into a final song.

A **single** is just one song released on its own.

A **release** is when a piece of music (or anything else someone makes) is put out into the world for sale.

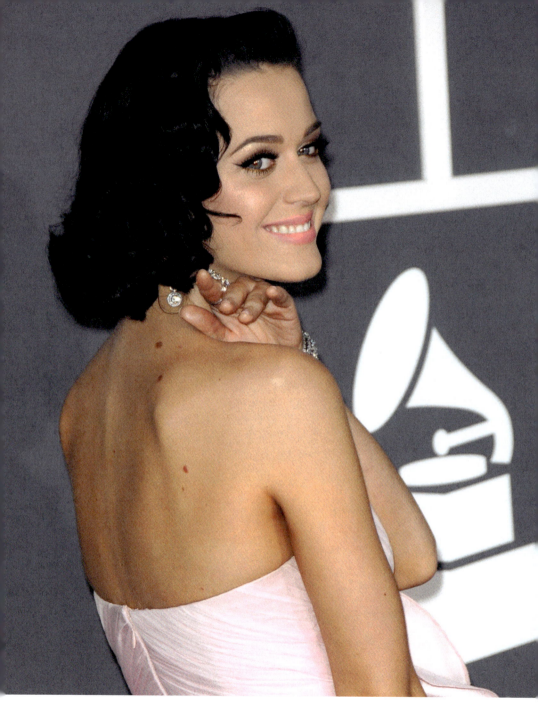

When Katy made it to the Grammys in 2009, she had already come further than most musicians come in a lifetime—but she would attend many more Grammy Awards in years to come.

believe she had finally found success! Her singles became smash hits, selling millions of downloads and playing on every radio station. Her first album had delivered some amazing music—but Katy was far from finished.

At the 2009 Grammy Awards show, Katy performed her hit "I Kissed a Girl." The performance was proof that Katy had earned a place in the music business. And the millions of people watching the Grammys allowed Katy to reach even more people with her music and unique style.

At the end of 2009, Katy released an album of her performance on the MTV show MTV Unplugged. The show is famous for bringing on artists to play their songs with a live band. The performance let Katy show off her guitar playing and singing in a different way from how many fans had seen the singer before. The album gave people a chance to listen to the performance whenever they wanted. After the success of Katy's album *One of the Boys*, her MTV Unplugged album was another great way for fans to hear more from the new princess of pop. And soon, fans would be getting much more music from the superstar singer.

# Find Out Even More

Reading books is one way to learn more about musicians like Katy Perry. Going on the Internet is another great way to learn even more details about Katy.

Finding information online can be overwhelming—there's no author to pick what information is important and what isn't. You won't find everything organized into a story that makes sense from start to finish. Instead, you may have to put the facts together for yourself.

Search engines are often the best place to start looking for facts online. Search engines like Google or Bing help to narrow down all the information on the Internet and give you the best sources of information for what you want to find. Keywords are the way to use search engines. These are words—or groups of words—that tell the search engines what you're looking for. It's not always as simple as it sounds, though.

Type "Nashville" into Google, for example, and you'll get more than 52 million results. If you're hoping to find out more about Katy Perry, you'll need to narrow down your search. Next you might try entering Katy Perry's name AND Nashville as keywords. But then you'll see lots of sites advertising where you can buy tickets to Katy's upcoming concerts in Nashville. That's not what you want either! You'll need to think about what you really want to know. In this case, maybe you're hoping to find out more about how Katy got her start in music. If you use "Katy Perry," "early years," and "Nashville" as your keywords, you'll get what you're looking for.

Try searching using more keywords, such as these:

Katy Perry childhood
Katy Perry teen years
Katy Perry's family
Katy Perry's religious beliefs (This will get you information about what Katy believes today—which is pretty different from what she was raised to believe!)

# Chapter Three

# Katy Becomes a Superstar

After the amazing success of Katy's first album, some people wondered whether she could continue to stay popular. Could she deliver more songs as catchy as "Hot N Cold" and "I Kissed a Girl"? With her second album, *Teenage Dream*, Katy proved she could!

## TEENAGE DREAM

Katy told MTV News that before she recorded her new album she wanted to get back to her roots. She left Los Angeles and went back to Santa Barbara. While she was back in her hometown, she started working on the songs that would become number-one hits, including "Firework" and "Teenage Dream." These songs would shape her second album and become huge hits for the singer.

Katy released *Teenage Dream* in August 2010. The album's first single, "California Gurls," is a fun song featuring rapper Snoop Dogg. In the song, Katy sings about what makes her home state so special. In the video for the song, Katy enters a

Rebecca Black, the singer of a popular YouTube song called "Friday," appeared in the music video for Katy Perry's "Last Friday Night."

dream world made of candy. The video fit perfectly with the fun, sweet sound of the song and Katy's exciting, colorful fashion. The song was a bit hit for Katy. People were starting to realize now that Katy wasn't just a one-album musician. She had what it takes to be a superstar!

"Teenage Dream" was the next single from the album of the same name. The song is about being young and in love. Like "California Gurls," "Teenage Dream" became a hit song. It reached number one on the Hot 100 chart. Katy's streak of amazing singles was still going strong!

Katy's next single, "Firework," was another huge success for the singer. Katy told MTV that the song was her favorite on *Teenage Dream*. "I hope this could be one of those [songs] where it's like, 'Yeah, I want to put my fist up and feel proud and feel strong,'" she said. By 2011, the song had been downloaded more than three million times. Katy's fans loved the song with its big sound.

*Teenage Dream* had more big hits. "E.T.," an alien-themed song featuring rapper Kanye West, was the next single. The song knocked Lady Gaga's "Born This Way" from the top spot on the *Billboard* Hot 100, making it Katy's fifth number-one song. "Last Friday Night (T.G.I.F.)" was still another number-one song for Katy. "The One That Got Away" is the only single from *Teenage Dream* that didn't reach the top of the chart, though the song did break into the top five.

Katy had amazing success with her album. Most of all, she had proven herself to be one of the biggest new voices in pop music. She was making hit after hit in a way that other artists only dream about. For Katy, pop music success seemed easy.

Few albums have the success of Katy's *Teenage Dream*. In the three years after it's release, the album sold more than 2.5

Katy and Russell Brand met when she appeared in his movie, *Get Him to the Greek*, in 2009. They married the following year.

## Music History: Gold and Platinum Albums

Since 1958, the Recording Industry Association of America (RIAA) has been awarding artists with gold and platinum records for high numbers of albums sold. The RIAA gives gold records to artists for 500,000 records sold, and platinum records for one million sold. Though the RIAA has been giving out the awards for more than five decades, the awards have changed over the years. At first, the awards were given based on the amount of money a song or album made instead of the number of sales. The RIAA's first award was gold, and then the platinum award was added in 1976. For more information about the RIAA's awards for artists, visit RIAA.com.

million copies in the United States. The Recording Industry Association of America (RIAA) awarded Katy's album a platinum twice (for sales over two million). Only Michael Jackson had more number-one songs from a single album than Katy did from *Teenage Dream*.

Katy had more happy things going on her life, besides her success. She had started dating British comedian Russell Brand in 2009, and by the end of the year, the two were engaged to be married. A year after that, in 2010, Katy and Russell were married in India.

## ANOTHER DREAM

After the success of *Teenage Dream*, Katy knew her fans wanted more. In 2012, Katy released a new version of her successful album, *Teenage Dream: The Complete Confection*. The new version had new songs and a few **remixes** to songs from the original album. "Part of Me" became a number-one hit when *The Complete Confection* came out.

The next single, "Wide Awake," didn't quite hit the top spot on the Hot 100 chart, but the song had special meaning for Katy. After all her success, it was time to tell fans the story behind the music. Her movie *Katy Perry: Part of Me* would do just that. She talked to MTV about how she wrote the song for the movie. "I love this song so much," she said. "It was a song that I hadn't written for *Teenage Dream*. I was doing this movie and they asked me if I wanted to write an end-title song for the movie and I was like, 'I know exactly what I want to say.' I was really kind of dying to write another song at that point. I didn't want to wait until I did a whole new record, and it's kind of the perfect last word of me at this moment."

**Remixes** are new versions of songs made by rearranging the sounds and parts of the song.

## KATY MAKES A MOVIE

Few pop stars get to make their own movie. But Katy is no ordinary pop star. *Katy Perry: Part of Me* gave fans an inside look at Katy's life and her live concerts. The movie gives the audience information about Katy's story growing up in a religious home in Santa Barbara. In the movie, Katy talks about her rise to success in the music business. For many fans, the movie is their first glimpse of Katy's real-life story.

It was also a chance to see Katy's concerts on the big screen. The movie shows many performances from the tour Katy did after *Teenage Dream*. In her concerts, Katy wears amazing costumes while performing on incredible stages made to look just like her fantastical music videos. Katy's concerts bring fans into her candy-colored world, and *Part of Me* gave fans who had never been to a Katy Perry concert the chance to see their favorite singer in a new way.

In the movie, Katy also talks about her divorce from Russell Brand. Just a few years after the two married, they split up. Katy says she was hurt by the breakup, but she knew that she and Russell wanted different things from their lives. Talking to MTV News, she also said it was important for her to keep going after the divorce, for herself and for others. "[If] I can be an example showing people that they don't have to lay down and die because they've been thrown a curveball, then that's great," Katy said. "If I can help someone else out because they feel like the only loner in the world or the only person that is going through the situation and they see me and they're inspired to keep moving forward, then I've done my job."

Katy also said she wanted to make sure fans saw the good and the bad of her life in *Part of Me*—her success as well as the sadness of her breakup. For Katy, it was important to be honest about her life with her fans.

With *Teenage Dream* and her own movie, Katy was proving she was one of the most important people in music, a true superstar. Many artists work their entire lives for one number-one hit. Katy had seven by the end of 2012. Katy's next album would add to that number!

# Find Out Even More

When you're searching for information online using search engines like Google, you'll find more websites than you could possibly read. Take a look at the list below to see just a few of the websites Google will find for you if you search for "Katy Perry."

**Katy Perry: Home**
www.katyperry.com
**Katy Perry - Wikipedia, the free encyclopedia**
en.wikipedia.org/wiki/Katy_Perry
**Katy Perry (katyperry) on Twitter**
https://twitter.com/katyperry
**Katy Perry | New Music And Songs | MTV**
www.mtv.com/artists/katy-perry
**Katy Perry : People.com**
www.people.com/people/katy_perry
**Katy Perry | Facebook**
https://www.facebook.com/katyperry

Google will find millions of websites for almost any musical artist or song you search for. But not every result you find using search engines will have exactly what you want. Can you tell which of the websites listed here is most likely to have the best information about Katy Perry's life and music?

Katy Perry's official website is katyperry.com. That means it's the website that Katy says was made with her approval. An official website is the usually the best place to find news and information about your favorite singers and musicians. When you visit an artist's official page, you can be sure that the information you're reading is coming straight from the artist herself.

Wikipedia can be a good place to read about many subjects, including music stars like Katy Perry. Keep in mind, though, that anyone can post information about any topic they want on Wikipedia. Artists like Katy don't control the information people post about them on Wikipedia. Be sure to read the source of the information you see on the site by clicking the small number next to any fact you want to check. If you don't see any number after a fact, it might not really be true!

When you use the Internet to learn more about something—whether it's Katy Perry or a topic for a school report—keep in mind that not everything you read online is true. Check out the websites you use. Who created them? (Is it someone who has reason to know about the topic? Or is it someone who might be making up facts?) Why were the sites created? (If a site was created to sell something, the facts on it may be intended to make you buy something. They may be true—but they could be exaggerated or even made up. There's nothing that keeps people from lying on the Internet!) When was the last time the sites were updated? (Sites that aren't updated regularly may contain old information that is no longer true.)

## Chapter Four

# Katy Today

Katy's *Teenage Dream* had been a huge success. The album sold millions and showed fans around the world that Katy could give them more and more great music. Katy had come a long way from the life she was living as a little girl in Santa Barbara.

Now she was **touring** the world and touching millions of lives with her music. Her songs were playing on the radio and her videos were watched by millions of people on the Internet. With her next album, she continued her amazing streak of success.

> **Touring** is when a musician puts on a lot of concerts in various locations around the country or even around the world, traveling from one to the next.

### PRISM

With her very public divorce and all the hard work that had gone into her success, Katy had been through a lot in just a few years. She decided to take some time off from music after

Being a voice actor in *The Smurfs 2* was a new experience for Katy. Although the film didn't do that well, she was glad to have the experience!

her movie *Katy Perry: Part of Me*. She tried something new and voiced the part of Smurfette in *The Smurfs 2*. Katy talked to news agency Reuters about the time between recording *Teenage Dream* and making her new album *Prism*. "I went through a lot of experiences in my life that I think built more character," Katy told Reuters. "I had to find my own self-identity the hard way. But I did. I came out alive and stronger, a little bit stronger."

Fans were hungry for new music from their favorite pop star. Katy didn't disappoint them. With her new album, Katy was back. She released her album *Prism* in October 2013.

Fans were introduced to the first single from the album with Katy's boxing performance at the 2013 MTV VMAs. "Roar" went on to be another number-one song for Katy, but it was just the first from *Prism*. After the success of "Roar," Katy followed up with "Unconditionally," an emotional love song.

With "Dark Horse," Katy changed her style completely. "Dark Horse" features rapper Juicy J and a beat that wouldn't be out of place on a rap album. For Katy, the song was different, but it allowed her to reach even greater heights. "Dark Horse" became the second number-one song from *Prism*, and Katy's ninth number-one song. Katy talked to *Billboard* magazine about the success of the song: "This number one is the most unexpected one I've ever had. I'm so thrilled and grateful to have these moments." Katy also performed the song with Juicy J at the 2014 Grammy Awards, helping the song to reach the top spot on *Billboard*'s Hot 100 pop song chart. Dressed in dark purple, black, and red, she gave a creepy and powerful performance of the song.

*Prism* is the latest in a line of blockbuster albums from Katy. In the first week, the album sold more than 250,000 copies. By

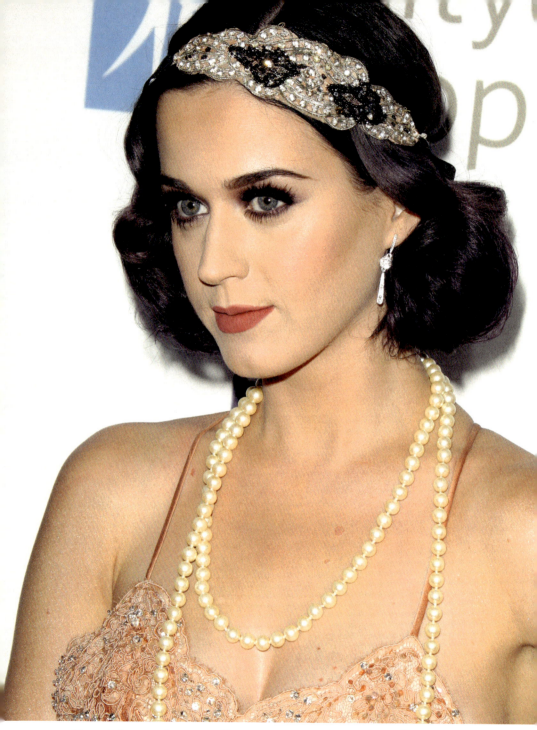

Katy is known for more than just music. She is also influential in fashion and for her work as an activist.

## The Business of Katy Perry

Katy has been on *Forbes* magazine's list of top-earning celebrities for years. The pop singer has made her art into a successful music business. Today, very few musical artists make as much money as Katy does from touring, song and album sales, as well as money from her movie, *Katy Perry: Part of Me*. Katy has proven that she's got the songs to stick around on radio and the fans to make her one of music's most successful stars.

the end of the year, the album had sold well over 2.5 million copies around the world.

# KATY'S WORK OUTSIDE MUSIC

Katy's not only a successful pop star. She's also a business-woman who has worked with companies like H&M, Adidas, and Proactiv. She has her own perfumes, Purr, Meow!, and Killer Queen that have all sold well. Katy even has her own version of the popular Sims video game, *Sims 3: Katy Perry's Sweet Treats*.

Katy is also an **activist** who works hard for causes she believes in. She's fighting bullying; she works for AIDS/HIV research, as well as education; she's

An **activist** is someone working to make the world a better place.

given **charity** concerts for causes such as cancer research; and she's doing what she can to get people to protect the environment. She's generous with her time and money, donating proceeds from some of her songs to groups that help artists in poor and rural areas, as well as to UNICEF and other charitable causes. When Katy went on the California Dreams Tour in 2011, for example, she sold out 124 arenas around the globe—and a portion of the money from every ticket was donated to the Children's Health Fund, Generosity Water, and the Humane Society. Part of **merchandise** sales was donated to the Red Cross to benefit local disaster relief efforts.

One of the causes that Katy cares about most is **LGBT** rights. She's worked with the Trevor Project and the It Gets Better campaign to reach out to LGBT young people. She's also spoken out in favor of **marriage equality**. Katy told DoSomething.org about how her opinions on LGBT rights changed over time. "I've come a long way from where I was raised, and I think specifically I realized that when I moved out of my home and I started meeting lots of different types of people," she told the website. Today, Katy lets her fans know how important equality—for everyone—is to her.

## LOOKING TO THE FUTURE

Since her 2008 album *One of the Boys*, Katy Perry has taken over the music world. She's sold millions of albums and earned millions of fans. Her songs are hits around the world. Katy has had more success in music in just a short time than most other artists can reach in a lifetime. The girl who grew up in a religious home that didn't allow pop music, today is one of pop's biggest stars.

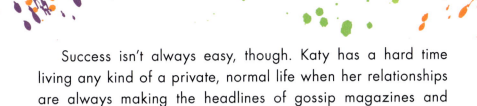

Success isn't always easy, though. Katy has a hard time living any kind of a private, normal life when her relationships are always making the headlines of gossip magazines and websites. Part of being a superstar is having the world pay attention to even the smallest things you do. That means your mistakes get noticed and talked about!

Katy doesn't let the gossip get her down, though. Through it all, she keeps giving her fans amazing music that they love. Her career is just beginning—and her fans are waiting to sing along with her next number-one hit!

**Charity** is when the money made from something is donated to those in need.

**Merchandise** is the goods you can buy at an event, like t-shirts and CDs.

**LGBT** means lesbian, gay, bisexual, and transgender, as well as the community and rights of anyone who fits that description.

**Marriage equality** is the belief that all people should be able to marry whoever they want, and their marriages should be treated the same as those between a man and a woman.

# Find Out Even More

The Internet has information on pretty much every topic in the world, including Katy Perry's life and music—but it can be hard to find exactly the information you want. Here are a few of pointers that will help you the next time you use the Internet for research:

• If you're using Google, after you get the results from you keywords, look at the very bottom of the page. You'll find there a list of other searches that are related to yours. These can give you ideas about how to narrow down your searches. For example, if you use "Katy Perry" as your keywords, the related searches at the bottom of the page will be all of these:

> katy perry songs
> katy perry firework
> katy perry wide awake
> katy perry russell brand
> katy perry hot n cold
> katy perry song list
> katy perry divorce
> katy perry tour

- If you're using Bing as your search engine, you might want to do a visual search to find what you want. Bing uses more pictures than other search engines, which can be a big help if your typing or spelling skills aren't the greatest.

- Adding more keywords to your search will help narrow down the sites that come up. So what, exactly, do you want to know about Katy? If you want to know about her charity work, for example, use "Katy Perry charities" as your keywords. But what if you want to know about just the charities she's helped this year—or her work with one specific charity? Then you could add more keywords, like a date or the name of a charity. Your new search might be "Katy Perry charities 2014"—or "Katy Perry charities UNICEF."

- If you're using Google, if you put quotation marks around a set of words, it will direct Google to search for those exact words, in that exact order. If you're searching for some of Katy's song lyrics, this is a great tool to use.

# Here's What We Recommend

## IN BOOKS

Adams, Michelle Medlock. *Katy Perry (Blue Banner Biographies)*. Hockessin, DE: Mitchell Lane Publishers, 2011.

Higgins, Nadia. *Katy Perry: From Gospel Singer to Pop Star (Pop Culture Bios)*. Minneapolis, MN.: Lerner Publishing Group, 2012.

Johnson, Robin. *Katy Perry (Superstars!)*. Mankato, MN.: Crabtree Publishing Company, 2011.

Tieck, Sarah. *Katy Perry: Singing Sensation (Big Buddy Biographies)*. Minneapolis, MN.: Abdo Publishing Group, 2011.

## ONLINE

Katy Perry's Official Twitter (@katyperry)
twitter.com/katyperry

Katy Perry's Official Website
www.katyperry.com

Katy Perry on Billboard.com
www.billboard.com/artist/305595/katy-perry

Katy Perry on Grammy.com
www.grammy.com/artist/katy-perry

Katy Perry on MTV.com
www.mtv.com/artists/katy-perry

# Index

# About the Author

C.F. Earl is a writer living and working in Binghamton, New York. Earl writes on a range of topics, including pop culture, history, and health.

# Picture Credits

**Dreamstime.com:**

6: Sbukley

10: Dave Newman

14: Simonwedege

18: Aaron Settipane

20: Sbukley

24: Featureflash

26: Featureflash

28: Sbukley

34: Featureflash

36: Sbukley

38: Carrienelson1

Made in the USA
Middletown, DE
18 February 2019